John Muir's

Book
Of
Animals

John Muir's

Book of Animals

John Muir

Illustrations by Lisel Jane Ashlock

Heyday, Berkeley, California

The Heyday Future Fund generously supported this book.

Library of Congress Cataloging-in-Publication Data
Muir, John, 1838-1914
John Muir's book of animals / John Muir ; illustrations by Lisel Jane Ashlock.
    pages cm
Summary: Peppered throughout famed naturalist John Muir's published work, articles, and letters and journals are wonderful descriptions of animals and stories about his encounters with them. -- From publisher.
ISBN 978-1-59714-318-9 (pbk. : alk. paper)
    1. Wildlife watching--United States. 2. Forest animals--United States. 3. Animals--United States. 4. Habitat (Ecology)--United States. 5. Muir, John, 1838-1914. I. Title. II. Title: Book of animals.
QL155.M85 2015
590.72'34--dc23
                            2015000565

Text Selection: Gayle Wattawa
Cover Art: Lisel Jane Ashlock
Book Design: Ashley Ingram

Orders, inquiries, and correspondence should be addressed to:
    Heyday
    P.O. Box 9145, Berkeley, CA 94709
    (510) 549-3564, Fax (510) 549-1889
    www.heydaybooks.com

Printed in Visalia, CA by Jostens

10 9 8 7 6 5 4 3 2 1

Any glimpse into the life of an animal quickens our own and makes it so much larger and better in every way.

JOHN MUIR

Contents

ANT   1
BEAR   7
BEE   13
CLARKE CROW   17
DEER   23
DOG   29
EAGLE AND HARE   33
GOLDEN EAGLE   35
GOOSE   39
GRASSHOPPER   43
GROUSE   47
HERON   53
LIZARD   57
MOUSE   61
RATTLESNAKE   65
RAVEN   73
SALMON   77
DOMESTIC SHEEP   79
WILD SHEEP   85
SONGBIRD   91
SPARROW   97
SQUIRREL   101
DOUGLAS SQUIRREL   105
WATER OUZEL   109
WOLF   113
WOOD RAT   117
WOODCHUCK   121
SOURCES   124

ANT

Mastodons and elephants used to live here no great geological time ago, as shown by their bones, often discovered by miners in washing gold-gravel. And bears of at least two species are here now, besides the California lion or panther, and wild cats, wolves, foxes, snakes, scorpions, wasps, tarantulas; but one is almost tempted at times to regard a small savage black ant as the master existence of this vast mountain world. These fearless, restless, wandering imps, though only about a quarter of an inch long, are fonder of fighting and biting than any beast I know. They attack every living thing around their homes, often without cause as far as I can see. Their bodies are mostly jaws curved like ice-hooks, and to get work for these weapons seems to be their chief aim and pleasure. Most of their colonies are established in living oaks somewhat decayed or hollowed, in which they can conveniently build their cells. These are chosen probably because of their strength as opposed to the attacks of animals and storms. They work both day and night, creep into dark caves, climb the highest trees, wander and hunt through cool ravines as well as on hot, unshaded ridges, and extend their highways and byways over everything but water and sky. From the foothills to a mile above the level of the sea nothing can stir without their knowledge; and alarms are spread in an incredibly short time, without any howl or cry that we can hear. I can't understand the need of their ferocious courage; there seems to be no common sense in it. Sometimes, no doubt, they fight in defense of their homes, but they fight anywhere and always wherever they can find anything to bite. As soon as a vulnerable spot is discovered on man or beast, they stand on their heads and sink their jaws, and though torn limb from limb, they will yet hold on and die biting deeper. When I contemplate this fierce creature so widely distributed and strongly entrenched, I see that much remains to be done ere the world is brought under the rule of universal peace and love.

On my way to camp a few minutes ago, I passed a dead pine nearly ten feet in diameter. It has been

enveloped in fire from top to bottom so that now it
looks like a grand black pillar set up as a monument.
In this noble shaft a colony of large jet-black ants have
established themselves, laboriously cutting tun-
nels and cells through the wood, whether sound
or decayed. The entire trunk seems to have been
honeycombed, judging by the size of the talus
of gnawed chips like sawdust piled up around its base.
They are more intelligent looking than their small,
belligerent, strong-scented brethren, and have better
manners, though quick to fight when required. Their
towns are carved in fallen trunks as well as in those
left standing, but never in sound, living trees or in the
ground. When you happen to sit down to rest or take
notes near a colony, some wandering hunter is sure
to find you and come cautiously forward to discover
the nature of the intruder and what ought to be done.
If you are not too near the town and keep perfectly
still he may run across your feet a few times, over your
legs and hands and face, up your trousers, as if taking your measure and getting comprehensive views,
then go in peace without raising an alarm. If, however, a tempting spot is offered or some suspicious

When I contemplate
this fierce creature so
widely distributed and strongly
entrenched, I see that much
remains to be done ere the world
is brought under the rule of
universal peace and love.

movement excites him, a bite follows, and such a bite! I fancy that a bear or wolf bite is not to be compared with it. A quick electric flame of pain flashes along the outraged nerves, and you discover for the first time how great is the capacity for sensation you are possessed of. A shriek, a grab for the animal, and a bewildered stare follow this bite of bites as one comes back to consciousness from sudden eclipse. Fortunately, if careful, one need not be bitten oftener than once or twice in a lifetime. This wonderful electric species is about three fourths of an inch long. Bears are fond of them, and tear and gnaw their home-logs to pieces, and roughly devour the eggs, larvae, parent ants, and the rotten or sound wood of the cells, all in one spicy acid hash....Thus are the poor biters bitten, like every other biter, big or little, in the world's great family.

BEAR

In my first interview with a Sierra bear we were frightened and embarrassed, both of us, but the bear's behavior was better than mine. When I discovered him, he was standing in a narrow strip of meadow, and I was concealed behind a tree on the side of it. After studying this appearance as he stood at rest, I rushed toward him to frighten him, that I might study his gait in running. But, contrary to all I had heard about the shyness of bears, he did not run at all; and when I stopped short within a few steps of him, as he held his ground in a fighting attitude, my mistake was monstrously plain. I was then put on my good behavior, and never afterward forgot the right manners of the wilderness.

This happened on my first Sierra excursion in the forest to the north of Yosemite Valley. I was eager to meet the animals, and many of them came to me as if willing to show themselves and make my acquaintance; but the bears kept out of my way.

An old mountaineer, in reply to my questions, told me that bears were very shy, all save grim old grizzlies, and that I might travel the mountains for years without seeing one, unless I gave my mind to them and practiced the stealthy ways of hunters. Nevertheless, it was only a few weeks after I had received this information that I met the one mentioned above, and obtained instruction at first hand.

I was encamped in the woods about a mile back of the rim of Yosemite, beside a stream that falls into the valley by the way of Indian Canyon. Nearly every day for weeks I went to the top of the North Dome to sketch; for it commands a general view of the valley, and I was anxious to draw every tree and rock and waterfall. Carlo, a Saint Bernard dog, was my companion—a fine, intelligent fellow that belonged to a hunter who was compelled to remain all summer on the hot plains, and who loaned him to me for the season for the sake of having him in the mountains, where he would be so much better off. Carlo knew bears through long experience, and he it was who led me to my first interview, though he seemed as much surprised as the bear at my unhunter-like behavior. One morning in June, just as the sunbeams began to stream through the trees, I set out for a day's sketching on the dome; and before we had gone half a mile from camp Carlo snuffed the air and looked cautiously ahead, lowered his bushy tail, drooped his ears, and began to step softly like a cat, turning every few yards and looking me in the face with a telling expression, saying plainly enough, "There is a bear a little way ahead." I walked carefully in the indicated direction, until I approached a small flowery meadow that I was familiar with, then crawled to the foot of a tree on its margin, bearing in mind what I had been told about the shyness of bears. Looking out cautiously over the instep of the tree, I saw a big, burly cinnamon bear about thirty yards off, half erect, his paws resting on the trunk of a fir that had fallen into the meadow, his hips almost buried in grass and flowers. He was listening attentively and trying to catch the scent, showing that in some way he was aware of our approach. I watched his gestures, and tried to make the most of my opportunity to learn what I could about him, fearing he would not stay long. He made a fine picture, standing alert in the sunny garden walled in by the most beautiful firs in the world.

After examining him at leisure, noting the sharp muzzle thrust inquiringly forward, the long shaggy hair on his broad chest, the stiff ears nearly buried in hair, and the slow, heavy way in which he moved his head, I foolishly made a rush on him, throwing up my arms and shouting to frighten him, to see him run. He did not mind the demonstration much; only pushed his head farther forward, and looked at me sharply as if asking, "What now? If you want to fight, I'm ready." Then I began to fear that on me would fall the work of running. But I was afraid to run, lest he should be encouraged to pursue me; therefore I held my ground, staring him in the face within a dozen yards or so, putting on as bold a look as I could, and hoping the influence of the human eye would be as great as it is said to be. Under these strained relations the interview seemed to last a long time. Finally, the bear, seeing how still I was, calmly withdrew his huge paws from the log,

gave me a piercing look, as if warning me not to follow him, turned, and walked slowly up the middle
of the meadow into the forest; stopping every few
steps and looking back to make sure that I was not
trying to take him at a disadvantage in a rear attack.
I was glad to part with him, and greatly enjoyed
the vanishing view as he waded through the lilies
and columbines.

BEE

Sauntering in the Shasta bee-lands in the sun-days of
summer, one may readily infer the time of day from
the comparative energy of bee-movements alone—
drowsy and moderate in the cool of the morning,
increasing in energy with the ascending sun, and, at
high noon, thrilling and quivering in wild ecstasy,
then gradually declining again to the stillness of
night. In my excursions among the glaciers I occasionally meet bees that are hungry, like mountaineers
who venture too far and remain too long above the
bread-line; then they droop and wither like autumn
leaves. The Shasta bees are perhaps better fed than
any others in the Sierra. Their fieldwork is one perpetual feast; but, however exhilarating the sunshine
or bountiful the supply of flowers, they are always
dainty feeders. Humming-moths and hummingbirds
seldom set foot upon a flower, but poise on the wing in
front of it, and reach forward as if they were sucking

Bees, though as dainty
as they, hug their favorite
flowers with profound cordiality,
and push their blunt, polleny faces
against them, like babies on
their mother's bosom.

through straws. But bees, though as dainty as they, hug their favorite flowers with profound cordiality, and push their blunt, polleny faces against them, like babies on their mother's bosom. And fondly, too, with eternal love, does Mother Nature clasp her small bee-babies, and suckle them, multitudes at once, on her warm Shasta breast.

CLARKE CROW

Of all the birds of the high Sierra, the strangest, noisiest, and most notable is the Clarke crow (*Nucifraga columbiana*). He is a foot long and nearly two feet in extent of wing, ashy gray in general color, with black wings, white tail, and a strong, sharp bill, with which he digs into the pinecones for the seeds on which he mainly subsists. He is quick, boisterous, jerky, and irregular in his movements and speech, and makes a tremendously loud and showy advertisement of himself—swooping and diving in deep curves across gorges and valleys from ridge to ridge, alighting on dead spars, looking warily about him, and leaving his dry springy perches, trembling from the vigor of his kick as he launches himself for a new flight, screaming from time to time loud enough to be heard more than a mile in still weather. He dwells far back on the high storm-beaten margin of the forest, where the mountain pine, juniper, and hemlock grow wide apart on glacier pavements and domes and rough crumbling ridges, and the dwarf pine makes a low crinkled growth along the flanks of the summit peaks. In so open a region, of course, he is well seen. Everybody notices him, and nobody at first knows what to make of him. One guesses he must be a woodpecker; another a crow or some sort of jay, another a magpie. He seems to be a pretty thoroughly mixed and fermented compound of all these birds, has all their strength, cunning, shyness, thievishness, and wary, suspicious curiosity combined and condensed. He flies like a woodpecker, hammers dead limbs for insects, digs big holes in pinecones to get at the seeds, cracks nuts held between his toes, cries like a crow or Steller's jay—but in a far louder, harsher, and more forbidding tone of voice—and besides his crow caws and screams, has a great variety of small chatter talk, mostly uttered in a fault-finding tone. Like the magpie, he steals articles that can be of no use to him. Once when I made my camp in a grove at Cathedral Lake, I chanced to leave a cake of soap on the shore where I had been washing, and a few minutes afterward I saw my soap flying past me through the grove, pushed by a Clarke crow.

In winter, when the snow is deep, the cones of the mountain pines are empty, and the juniper, hemlock, and dwarf pine orchard buried, he comes down to glean seeds in the yellow pine forests, startling the grouse with his loud screams. But even in winter, in calm weather, he stays in his high mountain home, defying the bitter frost. Once I lay snowbound through a three days' storm at the timberline on Mount Shasta; and while the roaring snow-laden blast swept by, one of these brave birds came to my camp, and began hammering at the cones on the topmost branches of half-buried pines, without showing the slightest distress. I have seen Clarke crows feeding their young as early as June 19, at a height of more than ten thousand feet, when nearly the whole landscape was snow covered.

They are excessively shy, and keep away from the traveler as long as they think they are observed; but when one goes on without seeming to notice them, or sits down and keeps still, their curiosity speedily gets the better of their caution, and they come flying from tree to tree, nearer and nearer, and watch

I chanced to leave a
cake of soap on the shore
where I had been washing, and
a few minutes afterward I
saw my soap flying past
me through the grove.

every motion. Few, I am afraid, will ever learn to like this bird, he is so suspicious and self-reliant, and his voice is so harsh that to most ears the scream of the eagle will seem melodious compared with it. Yet the mountaineer who has battled and suffered and struggled must admire his strength and endurance— the way he faces the mountain weather, cleaves the icy blasts, cares for his young, and digs a living from the stern wilderness.

DEER

Deer are capital mountaineers, making their way into the heart of the roughest mountains; seeking not only pasturage, but a cool climate, and safe hidden places in which to bring forth their young. They are not supreme as rock-climbing animals; they take second rank, yielding the first to the mountain sheep, which dwell above them on the highest crags and peaks. Still, the two meet frequently; for the deer climbs all the peaks save the lofty summits above the glaciers, crossing piles of angular boulders, roaring swollen streams, and sheer-walled canyons by fords and passes that would try the nerves of the hardiest mountaineers—climbing with graceful ease and reserve of strength that cannot fail to arouse admiration. Everywhere some species of deer seems to be at home—on rough or smooth ground, lowlands or highlands, in swamps and barrens and the densest woods, in varying climates, hot or cold, over all the continent;

maintaining glorious health, never making an awkward step. Standing, lying down, walking, feeding, running even for life, it is always invincibly graceful, and adds beauty and animation to every landscape—a charming animal, and a great credit to nature.

I never see one of the common blacktail deer, the only species in the Park [Yosemite National Park], without fresh admiration; and since I never carry a gun I see them well: lying beneath a juniper or dwarf pine, among the brown needles on the brink of some cliff or the end of a ridge commanding a wide outlook; feeding in sunny openings among chaparral, daintily selecting aromatic leaves and twigs; leading their fawns out of my way, or making them lie down and hide; bounding past through the forest, or curiously advancing and retreating again and again....

While exploring the upper canyon of the north fork of the San Joaquin, one evening, the sky threatening rain, I searched for a dry bed, and made choice of a big juniper that had been pushed down by a snow avalanche, but was resting stubbornly on its knees high enough to let me lie under its broad trunk. Just below my shelter there was another

juniper on the very brink of a precipice, and, examining it, I found a deer-bed beneath it, completely
protected and concealed by drooping branches—a
fine refuge and lookout as well as resting-place.
About an hour before dark I heard the clear, sharp
snorting of a deer, and looking down on the brushy,
rocky canyon bottom, discovered an anxious doe
that no doubt had her fawns concealed nearby. She
bounded over the chaparral and up the farther slope
of the wall, often stopping to look back and listen—a
fine picture of vivid, eager alertness. I sat perfectly still, and as my shirt was colored like the juniper
bark I was not easily seen. After a little she came
cautiously toward me, sniffing the air and grazing,
and her movements, as she descended the canyon
side over boulder piles and brush and fallen timber, were admirably strong and beautiful; she never
strained or made apparent efforts, although jumping
high here and there. As she drew nigh she sniffed
anxiously, trying the air in different directions until
she caught my scent; then bounded off, and vanished
behind a small grove of firs. Soon she came back
with the same caution and insatiable curiosity—

Standing, lying down, walking, feeding, running even for life, it is always invincibly graceful, and adds beauty and animation to every landscape.

coming and going five or six times. While I sat admiring her, a Douglas squirrel, evidently excited by her noisy alarms, climbed a boulder beneath me, and witnessed her performances as attentively as I did, while a risky chipmunk, too restless or hungry for such shows, busied himself about his supper in a thicket of shadbushes, the fruit of which was then ripe, glancing about on the slender twigs lightly as a sparrow.

DOG

None of us was able to make out what Stickeen was really good for. He seemed to meet danger and hardships without anything like reason, insisted on having his own way, never obeyed an order, and the hunter could never set him on anything, or make him fetch the birds he shot. His equanimity was so steady it seemed due to want of feeling; ordinary storms were pleasures to him, and as for mere rain, he flourished in it like a vegetable. No matter what advances you might make, scarce a glance or a tail-wag would you get for your pains. But though he was apparently as cold as a glacier and about as impervious to fun, I tried hard to make his acquaintance, guessing there must be something worthwhile hidden beneath so much courage, endurance, and love of wild-weathery adventure. No superannuated mastiff or bulldog grown old in office surpassed this fluffy midget in stoic dignity. He sometimes reminded me of a small, squat, unshakable

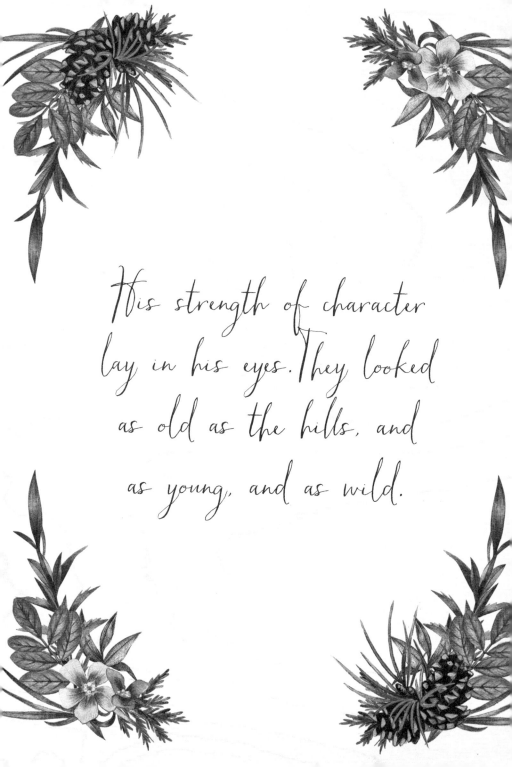

His strength of character
lay in his eyes. They looked
as old as the hills, and
as young, and as wild.

desert cactus. For he never displayed a single trace of the merry, tricksy, elfish fun of the terriers and collies that we all know, nor of their touching affection and devotion. Like children, most small dogs beg to be loved and allowed to love; but Stickeen seemed a very Diogenes, asking only to be let alone: a true child of the wilderness, holding the even tenor of his hidden life with the silence and serenity of nature. His strength of character lay in his eyes. They looked as old as the hills, and as young, and as wild. I never tired of looking into them: it was like looking into a landscape; but they were small and rather deep set, and had no explaining lines around them to give out particulars. I was accustomed to look into the faces of plants and animals, and I watched the little sphinx more and more keenly as an interesting study. But there is no estimating the wit and wisdom concealed and latent in our lower fellow mortals until made manifest by profound experiences; for it is through suffering that dogs as well as saints are developed and made perfect.

EAGLE AND HARE

The eagle does not dwell in the Hollow [Twenty Hill Hollow near Snelling, CA]; he only floats there to hunt the long-eared hare. One day I saw a fine specimen alight upon a hillside. I was at first puzzled to know what power could fetch the sky-king down into the grass with the larks. Watching him attentively, I soon discovered the cause of his earthiness. He was hungry and stood watching a long-eared hare, which stood erect at the door of his burrow, staring his winged fellow mortal full in the face. They were about ten feet apart. Should the eagle attempt to snatch the hare, he would instantly disappear in the ground. Should long-ears, tired of inaction, venture to skim the hill to some neighboring burrow, the eagle would swoop above him and strike him dead with a blow of his pinions, bear him to some favorite rock table, satisfy his hunger, wipe off all marks of grossness, and go again to the sky.

GOLDEN EAGLE

My Dear Sister Sarah:

To thee I give and bequeath this old gray quill with which I have written every word of my first book, knowing, as I do, your predilection for curiosities.

I can hardly remember its origin, but I think it is one that I picked up on the mountains, fallen from the wing of a golden eagle; but, possibly, it may be only a pinion feather of some tame old gray goose, and my love of truth compels me to make this unpoetical statement. The book that has grown from its whittled nib is, however, as wild as any that has ever appeared in these tame, civilized days. Perhaps I should have waited until the book was in print, for it is not absolutely certain that it will be accepted by the publishing houses. It has first to be submitted to the tasting critics, but as everything in the way of magazine and newspaper articles that the old pen has ever traced has been accepted and paid for, I reasonably hope I

I think it is one
that I picked up on the
mountains, fallen from the wing
of a golden eagle; but, possibly,
it may be only a pinion
feather of some tame
old gray goose.

shall have no difficulties in obtaining a publisher, The manuscript has just been sent to New York, and will be reported on in a few weeks. I leave for the mountains of Utah today.

The frayed upper end of the pen was produced by nervous gnawing when some interruption in my logic or rhetoric occurred from stupidity or weariness. I gnawed the upper end to send the thoughts below and out at the other.

Love to all your happy family and to thee and David. The circumstances of my life since I last bade you farewell have wrought many changes in me, but my love for you all has only grown greater from year to year, and whatsoever befalls I shall ever be,

Yours affectionately,

John Muir

GOOSE

The common gray goose, Canada honker, flying in regular harrow-shaped flocks, was one of the wildest and wariest of all the large birds that enlivened the spring and autumn. They seldom ventured to alight in our small lake [in Wisconsin], fearing, I suppose, that hunters might be concealed in the rushes; but on account of their fondness for the young leaves of winter wheat when they were a few inches high, they often alighted on our fields when passing on their way south, and occasionally even in our corn-fields when a snowstorm was blowing and they were hungry and wing-weary, with nearly an inch of snow on their backs. In such times of distress we used to pity them, even while trying to get a shot at them. They were exceedingly cautious and circum-spect; usually flew several times round the adjacent thickets and fences to make sure that no enemy was near before settling down, and one always stood on guard, relieved from time to time, while the flock was feeding. Therefore there was no chance to creep up on them unobserved; you had to be well hidden before the flock arrived. It was the ambition of boys to be able to shoot these wary birds. I never got but two, both of them at one so-called lucky shot. When I ran to pick them up, one of them flew away, but as the poor fellow was sorely wounded he didn't fly far. When I caught him after a short chase, he uttered a piercing cry of terror and despair, which the leader of the flock heard at a distance of about a hundred rods. They had flown off in frightened disorder, of course, but had got into the regular harrow-shape order when the leader heard the cry, and I shall never forget how bravely he left his place at the head of the flock and hurried back screaming and struck at me in trying to save his companion. I dodged down and held my hands over my head, and thus escaped a blow of his elbows. Fortunately, I had left my gun at the fence, and the life of this noble bird was spared after he had risked it in trying to save his wounded friend or neighbor or family relation. For so shy a bird boldly to attack a hunter showed wonderful sympathy and courage. This is one of my strangest hunting experiences. Never before had I regarded wild geese as dangerous, or capable of such noble self-sacrificing devotion.

GRASSHOPPER

A queer fellow and a jolly fellow is the grasshopper. Up the mountains he comes on excursions, how high I don't know, but at least as far and high as Yosemite tourists. I was much interested with the hearty enjoyment of the one that danced and sang for me on the Dome [Half Dome] this afternoon. He seemed brimful of glad, hilarious energy, manifested by springing into the air to a height of twenty or thirty feet, then diving and springing up again and making a sharp musical rattle just as the lowest point in the descent was reached. Up and down a dozen times or so he danced and sang, then alighted to rest, then up and at it again. The curves he described in the air in diving and rattling resembled those made by cords hanging loosely and attached at the same height at the ends, the loops nearly covering each other. Braver, heartier, keener, care-free enjoyment of life I have never seen or heard in any creature, great or small. The life of this comic redlegs, the mountain's merriest child, seems to be made up of pure, condensed gaiety. The Douglas squirrel is the only living creature that I can compare him with in exuberant, rollicking, irrepressible jollity. Wonderful that these sublime mountains are so loudly cheered and brightened by a creature so queer. Nature in him seems to be snapping her fingers in the face of all earthly dejection and melancholy with a boyish hip-hip-hurrah. How the sound is made I do not understand. When he was on the ground he made not the slightest noise, nor when he was simply flying from place to place, but only when diving in curves, the motion seeming to be required for the sound; for the more vigorous the diving the more energetic the corresponding outbursts of jolly rattling. I tried to observe him closely while he was resting in the intervals of his performances; but he would not allow a near approach, always getting his jumping legs ready to spring for immediate flight, and keeping his eyes on me. A fine sermon the little fellow danced for me on the Dome, a likely place to look for sermons in stones, but not for grasshopper sermons. A large and imposing pulpit for so small a preacher. No danger of weakness in the knees of the world while Nature can spring such a rattle as this. Even the bear did not express for me the mountain's wild health and strength and happiness so tellingly as did this comical little hopper. No cloud of care in his day, no winter of discontent in sight. To him every day is a holiday; and when at length his sun sets, I fancy he will cuddle down on the forest floor and die like the leaves and flowers, and like them leave no unsightly remains calling for burial.

GROUSE

Another magnificent bird, the blue or dusky grouse, next in size to the sage cock, is found all through the main forest belt [in Yosemite], though not in great numbers. They like best the heaviest silver-fir woods near garden and meadow openings, where there is but little underbrush to cover the approach of enemies. When a flock of these brave birds, sauntering and feeding on the sunny, flowery levels of some hidden meadow or Yosemite valley far back in the heart of the mountains, see a man for the first time in their lives, they rise with hurried notes of surprise and excitement and alight on the lowest branches of the trees, wondering what the wanderer may be, and showing great eagerness to get a good view of the strange vertical animal. Knowing nothing of guns, they allow you to approach within a half dozen paces, then quietly hop a few branches higher or fly to the next tree without a thought of concealment, so that you may observe them as long as you like, near enough to see the fine shading of their plumage, the feathers on their toes, and the innocent wonderment in their beautiful wild eyes. But in the neighborhood of roads and trails they soon become shy, and when disturbed fly into the highest, leafiest trees, and suddenly become invisible, so well do they know how to hide and keep still and make use of their protective coloring. Nor can they be easily dislodged ere they are ready to go. In vain the hunter goes round and round some tall pine or fir into which he has perhaps seen a dozen enter, gazing up through the branches, straining his eyes while his gun is held ready; not a feather can he see unless his eyes have been sharpened by long experience and knowledge of the blue grouse's habits. Then, perhaps, when he is thinking that the tree must be hollow and that the birds have all gone inside, they burst forth with a startling whir of wing-beats, and after gaining full speed go skating swiftly away through the forest arches in a long, silent, wavering slide, with wings held steady.

During the summer they are most of the time on the ground, feeding on insects, seeds, berries, etc., around the margins of open spots and rocky moraines, playing and sauntering, taking sun baths and sand baths, and drinking at little pools and rills during the heat of the day. In winter they live mostly in the trees, depending on buds for food, sheltering beneath dense overlapping branches at night and during storms on the leeside of the trunk, sunning themselves on the southside limbs in fine weather, and sometimes diving into the mealy snow to flutter and wallow, apparently for exercise and fun.

I have seen young broods running beneath the firs in June at a height of eight thousand feet above the sea. On the approach of danger, the mother with a peculiar cry warns the helpless midgets to scatter and hide beneath leaves and twigs, and even in plain open places it is almost impossible to discover them. In the meantime the mother feigns lameness, throws herself at your feet, kicks and gasps and flutters, to draw your attention from the chicks. The young are generally able to fly about the middle of July; but even after they can fly well they are usually advised to run and hide and lie still, no matter how closely approached, while the mother goes on with her loving, lying acting,

One touch of nature
makes the whole world kin;
and it is truly wonderful how
love-telling the small voices
of these birds are, and how far
they reach through the woods
into one another's hearts
and into ours.

apparently as desperately concerned for their safety as when they were featherless infants. Sometimes, however, after carefully studying the circumstances, she tells them to take wing; and up and away in a blurry birr and whir they scatter to all points of the compass, as if blown up with gunpowder, dropping cunningly out of sight three or four hundred yards off, and keeping quiet until called, after the danger is supposed to be past. If you walk on a little way without manifesting any inclination to hunt them, you may sit down at the foot of a tree near enough to see and hear the happy reunion. One touch of nature makes the whole world kin; and it is truly wonderful how love-telling the small voices of these birds are, and how far they reach through the woods into one another's hearts and into ours. The tones are so perfectly human and so full of anxious affection, few mountaineers can fail to be touched by them.

HERON

During my long sojourn here [at Cedar Keys] as a convalescent I used to lie on my back for whole days beneath the ample arms of these great trees, listening to the winds and the birds. There is an extensive shallow on the coast, close by, which the receding tide exposes daily. This is the feeding-ground of thousands of waders of all sizes, plumage, and language, and they make a lively picture and noise when they gather at the great family board to eat their daily bread, so bountifully provided for them.

Their leisure in time of high tide they spend in various ways and places. Some go in large flocks to reedy margins about the islands and wade and stand about quarrelling or making sport, occasionally finding a stray mouthful to eat. Some stand on the mangroves of the solitary shore, now and then plunging into the water after a fish. Some go long journeys inland, up creeks and inlets. A few lonely old herons of solemn

White-bearded hermits
gazing dreamily from dark
caves could not appear more
solemn or more becomingly
shrouded from the rest of
their fellow beings.

look and wing retire to favorite oaks. It was my delight to watch those old white sages of immaculate feather as they stood erect drowsing away the dull hours between tides, curtained by long skeins of tillandsia. White-bearded hermits gazing dreamily from dark caves could not appear more solemn or more becomingly shrouded from the rest of their fellow beings.

.

LIZARD

I slept at Turlock and next morning faced the
Sierra and set out through the sand afoot. The free-
dom I felt was exhilarating, and the burning heat
and thirst and faintness could not make it less.
Before I had walked ten miles I was wearied and
footsore, but it was real earnest work and I liked it.
Any kind of simple natural destruction is preferable
to the numb, dumb, apathetic deaths of a town....
Heavy wagon loads of wheat had been hauled
along the road and the wheels had sunk deep and
left smooth beveled furrows in the sand. Upon the
smooth slopes of these sand furrows I soon observed
a most beautiful and varied embroidery, evidently tracks of some kind. At first I thought of mice,
but soon saw they were too light and delicate for
mice. Then a tiny lizard darted into the stubble
ahead of me, and I carefully examined the track
he made, but it was entirely unlike the fine print

The riddle was solved.
I knew that mountain
boulders moved in music;
so also do lizards.

embroidery I was studying. However, I knew that he might make very different tracks if walking leisurely. Therefore I determined to catch one and experiment. I found out in Florida that lizards, however swift, are short-winded, so I gave chase and soon captured a tiny gray fellow and carried him to a smooth sand-bed where he could embroider without getting away into grass tufts or holes. He was so wearied that he couldn't skim and was compelled to walk, and I was excited with delight in seeing an exquisitely beautiful strip of embroidery about five-eighths of an inch wide, drawn out in flowing curves behind him as from a loom. The riddle was solved. I knew that mountain boulders moved in music; so also do lizards, and their written music, printed by their feet, moved so swiftly as to be invisible, covers the hot sands with beauty wherever they go.

MOUSE

When I was a boy in Scotland I was fond of everything that was wild, and all my life I've been growing
fonder and fonder of wild places and wild creatures.
Fortunately, around my native town of Dunbar, by
the stormy North Sea, there was no lack of wildness,
though most of the land lay in smooth cultivation....

My earliest recollections of the country
were gained on short walks with my grandfather when I was perhaps not over three years
old. On one of these walks Grandfather took me
to Lord Lauderdale's gardens, where I saw figs
growing against a sunny wall and tasted some of
them, and got as many apples to eat as I wished.
On another memorable walk in a hayfield, when
we sat down to rest on one of the haycocks I heard a
sharp, prickly, stinging cry, and, jumping up eagerly,
called Grandfather's attention to it. He said he heard
only the wind, but I insisted on digging into the hay

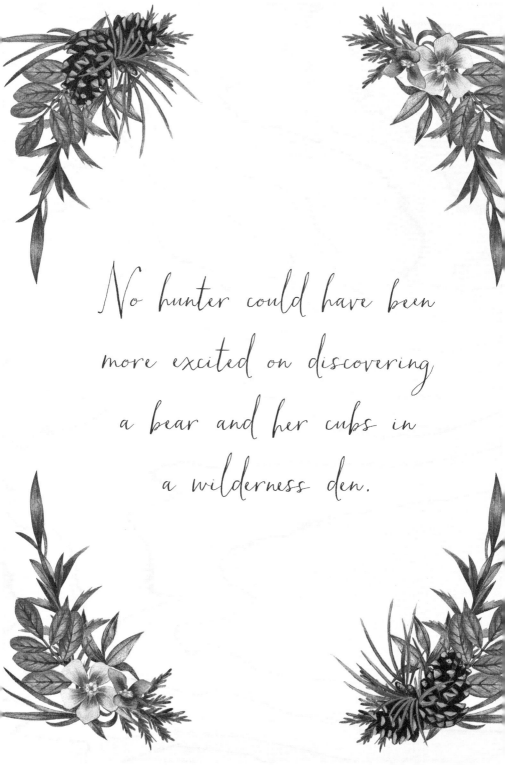

No hunter could have been
more excited on discovering
a bear and her cubs in
a wilderness den.

and turning it over until we discovered the source of the strange exciting sound—a mother field mouse with half a dozen naked young hanging to her teats. This to me was a wonderful discovery. No hunter could have been more excited on discovering a bear and her cubs in a wilderness den.

RATTLESNAKE

There are many snakes in the canyons and lower forests, but they are mostly handsome and harmless. Of all the tourists and travelers who have visited Yosemite and the adjacent mountains, not one has been bitten by a snake of any sort, while thousands have been charmed by them. Some of them vie with the lizards in beauty of color and dress patterns. Only the rattlesnake is venomous, and he carefully keeps his venom to himself as far as man is concerned, unless his life is threatened.

Before I learned to respect rattlesnakes I killed two, the first on the San Joaquin plain. He was coiled comfortably around a tuft of bunchgrass, and I discovered him when he was between my feet as I was stepping over him. He held his head down and did not attempt to strike, although in danger of being trampled. At that time, thirty years ago, I imagined that rattlesnakes should be killed wherever found.

I had no weapon of any sort, and on the smooth plain there was not a stick or a stone within miles; so I crushed him by jumping on him, as the deer are said to do. Looking me in the face he saw I meant mischief, and quickly cast himself into a coil, ready to strike in defense. I knew he could not strike when traveling, therefore I threw handfuls of dirt and grass sods at him, to tease him out of coil. He held his ground a few minutes, threatening and striking, and then started off to get rid of me. I ran forward and jumped on him; but he drew back his head so quickly my heel missed, and he also missed his stroke at me. Persecuted, tormented, again and again he tried to get away, bravely striking out to protect himself; but at last my heel came squarely down, sorely wounding him, and a few more brutal stampings crushed him. I felt degraded by the killing business, farther from heaven, and I made up my mind to try to be at least as fair and charitable as the snakes themselves, and to kill no more save in self-defense.

The second killing might also, I think, have been avoided, and I have always felt somewhat sore and guilty about it. I had built a little cabin in Yosemite,

and for convenience in getting water, and for the sake
of music and society, I led a small stream from Yosemite Creek into it. Running along the side of the wall
it was not in the way, and it had just fall enough to
ripple and sing in low, sweet tones, making delightful
company, especially at night when I was lying awake.
Then a few frogs came in and made merry with the
stream—and one snake, I suppose to catch the frogs.

Returning from my long walks, I usually brought
home a large handful of plants, partly for study,
partly for ornament, and set them in a corner of the
cabin, with their stems in the stream to keep them
fresh. One day, when I picked up a handful that
had begun to fade, I uncovered a large coiled rattler
that had been hiding behind the flowers. Thus suddenly brought to light face to face with the rightful
owner of the place, the poor reptile was desperately embarrassed, evidently realizing that he had
no right in the cabin. It was not only fear that he
showed, but a good deal of downright bashfulness
and embarrassment, like that of a more than half-
honest person caught under suspicious circumstances behind a door. Instead of striking or threatening to

He slowly drew his head down as far as he could, with awkward, confused kinks in his neck and a shamefaced expression, as if wishing the ground would open and hide him.

strike, though coiled and ready, he slowly drew his head down as far as he could, with awkward, confused kinks in his neck and a shamefaced expression, as if wishing the ground would open and hide him. I have looked into the eyes of so many wild animals that I feel sure I did not mistake the feelings of this unfortunate snake. I did not want to kill him, but I had many visitors, some of them children, and I oftentimes came in late at night; so I judged he must die.

Since then I have seen perhaps a hundred or more in these mountains, but I have never intentionally disturbed them, nor have they disturbed me to any great extent, even by accident, though in danger of being stepped on. Once, while I was on my knees kindling a fire, one glided under the arch made by my arm. He was only going away from the ground I had selected for a camp, and there was not the slightest danger, because I kept still and allowed him to go in peace. The only time I felt myself in serious danger was when I was coming out of the Tuolumne Canyon by a steep side canyon toward the head of Yosemite Creek. On an earthquake talus, a boulder in my way presented a front so high that I could just reach the upper edge of it while standing on the next below it. Drawing myself up, as soon as my head was above the flat top of it I caught sight of a coiled rattler. My hands had alarmed him, and he was ready for me; but even with this provocation, and when my head came in sight within a foot of him, he did not strike. The last time I sauntered through the big canyon I saw about two a day. One was not coiled, but neatly folded in a narrow space between two cobblestones on the side of the river, his head below the level of them, ready to shoot up like a jack-in-the-box for frogs or birds. My foot spanned the space above within an inch or two of his head, but he only held it lower. In making my way through a particularly tedious tangle of buckthorn, I parted the branches on the side of an open spot and threw my bundle of bread into it; and when, with my arms free, I was pushing through after it, I saw a small rattlesnake dragging his tail from beneath my bundle. When he caught sight of me he eyed me angrily, and with an air of righteous indignation seemed to be asking why I had thrown that stuff on him. He was so small that I was inclined to slight him, but he struck out so angrily that I drew back, and approached the opening from the other side. But he had been listening, and when I looked through the brush I found him confronting me, still with a come-in-if-you-dare expression. In vain I tried to explain that I only wanted my bread; he stoutly held the ground in front of it; so I went back a dozen rods and kept still for half an hour, and when I returned he had gone.

One evening, near sundown, in a very rough, boulder-choked portion of the canyon, I searched long for a level spot for a bed, and at last was glad to find a patch of flood-sand on the riverbank, and a lot of driftwood close by for a campfire. But when I threw down my bundle, I found two snakes in possession of the ground. I might have passed the night even in this snake den without danger, for I never knew a single instance of their coming into camp in the night; but fearing that, in so small a space, some latecomers, not aware of my presence, might get stepped on when I was replenishing the fire, to avoid possible crowding I encamped on one of the earthquake boulders.

RAVEN

July 15.

It has been a glorious day, all pure sunshine. An hour
or more before sunset the distant mountains, a vast
host, seemed more softly ethereal than ever, pale
blue, ineffably fine, all angles and harshness melted
off in the soft evening light. Even the snow and the
grinding, cascading glaciers became divinely tender and fine in this celestial amethystine light. I got
back to camp at 7:15, not tired. After my hardtack
supper I could have climbed the mountain again
and got back before sunrise, but dragging the sled
tires me. I have been out on the glacier examining a
moraine-like mass about a third of a mile from
camp. It is perhaps a mile long, a hundred yards
wide, and is thickly strewn with wood. I think that
it has been brought down the mountain by a heavy
snow avalanche, loaded on the ice, then carried
away from the shore in the direction of the flow of

the glacier. This explains detached moraine masses. This one seems to have been derived from a big roomy cirque or amphitheater on the northwest side of this Snow Dome Mountain.

To shorten the return journey I was tempted to glissade down what appeared to be a snow-filled ravine, which was very steep. All went well until I reached a bluish spot which proved to be ice, on which I lost control of myself and rolled into a gravel talus at the foot without a scratch. Just as I got up and was getting myself orientated, I heard a loud fierce scream, uttered in an exulting, diabolical tone of voice which startled me, as if an enemy, having seen me fall, was glorying in my death. Then suddenly two ravens came swooping from the sky and alighted on the jag of a rock within a few feet of me, evidently hoping that I had been maimed and that they were going to have a feast. But as they stared at me, studying my condition, impatiently waiting for bone-picking time, I saw what they were up to and shouted, "Not yet, not yet!"

July 16.

At 7:00 a.m. I left camp to cross the main glacier. Six ravens came to the camp as soon as I left. What wonderful eyes they must have! Nothing that moves in all this icy wilderness escapes the eyes of these brave birds. This is one of the loveliest mornings I ever saw in Alaska; not a cloud or faintest hint of one in all the wide sky. There is a yellowish haze in the east, white in the west, mild and mellow as a Wisconsin Indian Summer, but finer, more ethereal, God's holy light making all divine.

SALMON

As we neared the mouth of the well-known salmon-stream
where we intended making our camp, we noticed jets and
flashes of silvery light caused by the startled movement
of the salmon that were on their way to their spawn-
ing-grounds....The water about the canoe and beneath
the canoe was churned by thousands of fins into silver
fire....The stream was so filled with them there seemed to
be more fish than water in it, and we appeared to be sail-
ing in boiling, seething silver light marvelously relieved in
the jet darkness. In the midst of the general auroral glow
and the specially vivid flashes made by the frightened fish
darting ahead and to right and left of the canoe, our attention was suddenly fixed by a long, steady, comet-like blaze
that seemed to be made by some frightful monster that
was pursuing us. But when the portentous object reached
the canoe, it proved to be only our little dog, Stickeen.

DOMESTIC SHEEP

The drivers and dogs had a lively, laborious time getting the sheep across the creek, the second large stream thus far that they have been compelled to cross without a bridge....Men and dogs, shouting and barking, drove the timid, water-fearing creatures in a close crowd against the bank, but not one of the flock would launch away. While thus jammed, the Don and the shepherd rushed through the frightened crowd to stampede those in front, but this would only cause a break backward, and away they would scamper through the streambank trees and scatter over the rocky pavement. Then with the aid of the dogs the runaways would again be gathered and made to face the stream, and again the compacted mass would break away, amid wild shouting and barking that might well have disturbed the stream itself and marred the music of its falls, to which visitors no doubt from all quarters of the globe were listening. "Hold them there! Now hold them there!" shouted the Don; "the front ranks will soon tire of the pressure, and be glad to take to

the water, then all will jump in and cross in a hurry."
But they did nothing of the kind; they only avoided
the pressure by breaking back in scores and hundreds,
leaving the beauty of the banks sadly trampled.

If only one could be got to cross over, all would
make haste to follow; but that one could not be found.
A lamb was caught, carried across, and tied to a bush
on the opposite bank, where it cried piteously for its
mother. But though greatly concerned, the mother
only called it back. That play on maternal affection
failed, and we began to fear that we should be forced
to make a long roundabout drive and cross the widespread tributaries of the creek in succession. This
would require several days, but it had its advantages, for I was eager to see the sources of so famous a
stream. Don Quixote, however, determined that they
must ford just here, and immediately began a sort of
siege by cutting down slender pines on the bank and
building a corral barely large enough to hold the flock
when well pressed together. And as the stream would
form one side of the corral he believed that they could
easily be forced into the water.

In a few hours the inclosure was completed, and the silly animals were driven in and rammed hard against the brink of the ford.

Then the Don, forcing a way through the compacted mass, pitched a few of the terrified unfortunates into the stream by main strength; but instead of crossing over, they swam about close to the bank, making desperate attempts to get back into the flock. Then a dozen or more were shoved off, and the Don, tall like a crane and a good natural wader, jumped in after them, seized a struggling wether, and dragged it to the opposite shore. But no sooner did he let it go than it jumped into the stream and swam back to its frightened companions in the corral, thus manifesting sheep-nature as unchangeable as gravitation. Pan with his pipes would have had no better luck, I fear. We were now pretty well baffled. The silly creatures would suffer any sort of death rather than cross that stream. Calling a council, the dripping Don declared that starvation was now the only likely scheme to try, and that we might as well camp here in comfort and let the besieged flock grow hungry and cool, and come to their senses, if they had any. In a few minutes

I have seen fish
driven out of the water
with less ado than was
made in driving these
animals into it.

after being thus let alone, an adventurer in the foremost rank plunged in and swam bravely to the farther shore. Then suddenly all rushed in pell-mell together, trampling one another underwater, while we vainly tried to hold them back. The Don jumped into the thickest of the gasping, gurgling, drowning mass, and shoved them right and left as if each sheep was a piece of floating timber. The current also served to drift them apart; a long bent column was soon formed, and in a few minutes all were over and began baaing and feeding as if nothing out of the common had happened. That none were drowned seems wonderful. I fully expected that hundreds would gain the romantic fate of being swept into Yosemite over the highest waterfall in the world.

As the day was far spent, we camped a little way back from the ford, and let the dripping flock scatter and feed until sundown. The wool is dry now, and calm, cud-chewing peace has fallen on all the comfortable band, leaving no trace of the watery battle. I have seen fish driven out of the water with less ado than was made in driving these animals into it. Sheep brain must surely be poor stuff.

WILD SHEEP

While engaged in the work of exploring high regions where they [wild sheep] delight to roam I have been greatly interested in studying their habits. In the months of November and December, and probably during a considerable portion of midwinter, they all flock together, male and female, old and young. I once found a complete band of this kind numbering upward of fifty, which, on being alarmed, went bounding away across a jagged lava-bed at admirable speed, led by a majestic old ram, with the lambs safe in the middle of the flock.

In spring and summer, the full-grown rams form separate bands of from three to twenty, and are usually found feeding along the edges of glacier meadows, or resting among the castle-like crags of the high summits; and whether quietly feeding, or scaling the wild cliffs, their noble forms and the power and beauty of their movements never fail to strike the beholder with lively admiration.

Their resting places seem to be chosen with reference to sunshine and a wide outlook, and most of all to safety. Their feeding-grounds are among the most beautiful of the wild gardens, bright with daisies and gentians and mats of purple bryanthus, lying hidden away on rocky headlands and canyon sides, where sunshine is abundant, or down in the shady glacier valleys, along the banks of the streams and lakes, where the plushy sod is greenest. Here they feast all summer, the happy wanderers, perhaps relishing the beauty as well as the taste of the lovely flora on which they feed.

When the winter storms set in, loading their highland pastures with snow, then, like the birds, they gather and go to lower climates, usually descending the eastern flank of the range to the rough, volcanic table-lands and treeless ranges of the Great Basin adjacent to the Sierra. They never make haste, however, and seem to have no dread of storms, many of the strongest only going down leisurely to bare, wind-swept ridges, to feed on bushes and dry bunch-grass, and then returning up into the snow. Once I was snowbound on Mount Shasta for three days, a little below the timberline. It was a dark and stormy time, well calculated to test the skill and endurance of mountaineers. The snow-laden gale drove on night and day in hissing, blinding floods, and when at length it began to abate, I found that a small band of wild sheep had weathered the storm in the lee of a clump of dwarf pines a few yards above my storm-nest, where the snow was eight or ten feet deep. I was warm back of a rock, with blankets, bread, and fire. My brave companions lay in the snow, without food, and with only the partial shelter of the short trees, yet they made no sign of suffering or faintheartedness.

In the months of May and June, the wild sheep bring forth their young in solitary and almost inaccessible crags, far above the nesting-rocks of the eagle. I have frequently come upon the beds of the ewes and lambs at an elevation of from 12,000 to 13,000 feet above sea level. These beds are simply oval-shaped hollows, pawed out among loose, disintegrating rock-chips and sand, upon some sunny

Such is the cradle
of the little mountaineer,
aloft in the very sky;
rocked in storms, curtained
in clouds, sleeping in
thin, icy air.

spot commanding a good outlook, and partially shel-
tered from the winds that sweep those lofty peaks
almost without intermission. Such is the cradle of
the little mountaineer, aloft in the very sky; rocked
in storms, curtained in clouds, sleeping in thin, icy
air; but, wrapped in his hairy coat, and nourished by
a strong, warm mother, defended from the talons of
the eagle and the teeth of the sly coyote, the bonny
lamb grows apace. He soon learns to nibble the tufted
rock-grasses and leaves of the white spiraea; his horns
begin to shoot, and before summer is done he is strong
and agile, and goes forth with the flock, watched by
the same divine love that tends the more helpless
human lamb in its cradle by the fireside.

Nothing is more commonly remarked by noisy,
dusty trail-travelers in the Sierra than the want of
animal life—no songbirds, no deer, no squirrels, no
game of any kind, they say. But if such could only go
away quietly into the wilderness, sauntering afoot
and alone with natural deliberation, they would soon
learn that these mountain mansions are not without
inhabitants, many of whom, confiding and gentle,
would not try to shun their acquaintance.

SONGBIRD

Protect Our Songbirds
Some Action Should Be Taken Soon to Save the Warblers

If it be true that not a sparrow falls to the ground un-
noted, what cumbersome records must be piling up
to confront us! Watch the women that pass along the
street and you will be appalled at the crimes that are
committed in the name of vanity, for on nine hats out
of ten balance the fragments of a drawn and quar-
tered bird....If the half-starved dogs and superfluous
cats could be stuffed and used for millinery purposes,
women might decorate themselves to the uttermost
limits of their barbaric instincts, and not a protest
would be raised; but these poor little airships of nature, who earn their own living and contribute more
than their share to the beauty and harmony of the
world, must they go?

That is not a merely rhetorical question. They are going fast, and if we want to save them, something must be done about it. Orioles are nearly extinct in California, hummingbirds are growing scarcer every year, and all the tribes who have been cursed with bright plumage are swiftly diminishing. As though it were not enough to lose those, the sweetest singers of all birdland are being slaughtered by thousands to serve the ignoble purpose of an entree.

Love for songbirds, with their sweet human voices, appears to be more common and unfailing than love for flowers. Everyone loves flowers to some extent, at least in life's fresh morning, attracted by them as instinctively as hummingbirds and bees....One's first instinctive love of songbirds is never wholly obliterated, no matter what the influences upon our lives may be. I have often been delighted to see a pure, spiritual glow come into the countenances of hard businessmen and old miners, when a songbird chanced to alight near them. Nevertheless, the little mouthful of meat that swells out the breasts of some songbirds is too often the cause of their death....

An acquaintance of mine, a sort of foothill mountaineer, had a pet cat, a great, dozy, overgrown creature, about as broad-shouldered as a lynx. During the winter, while the snow lay deep, the mountaineer sat in his lonely cabin among the pines smoking his pipe and wearing the dull time away. Tom was his sole companion, sharing his bed, and sitting beside him on a stool with much the same drowsy expression of eye as his master. The good-natured bachelor was content with his hard fare of soda bread and bacon, but Tom, the only creature in the world acknowledging dependence on him, must needs be provided with fresh meat. Accordingly he bestirred himself to contrive squirrel traps, and waded the snowy woods with his gun, making sad havoc among the few winter birds, sparing neither robin, sparrow, nor tiny nuthatch, and the pleasure of seeing Tom eat and grow fat was his great reward.

One cold afternoon, while hunting along the riverbank, he noticed a plain-feathered little bird skipping about in the shallows, and immediately

Love for songbirds,
with their sweet human
voices, appears to be more
common and unfailing than
love for flowers.

raised his gun. But just then the confiding songster began to sing, and after listening to his summery melody the charmed hunter turned away, saying, "Bless your little heart, I can't shoot you, not even for Tom."

SPARROW

From early spring to late autumn [the little dun-headed sparrow] is to be found only on the snowy, icy peaks at the head of the glacier cirques and canyons [in Yosemite]. His feeding grounds in spring are the snow sheets between the peaks, and in midsummer and autumn the glaciers. Many bold insects go mountaineering almost as soon as they are born, ascending the highest summits on the mild breezes that blow in from the sea every day during steady weather; but comparatively few of these adventurers find their way down or see a flowerbed again. Getting tired and chilly, they alight on the snowfields and glaciers, attracted perhaps by the glare, take cold, and die. There they lie as if on a white cloth purposely outspread for them, and the dun sparrows find them a rich and varied repast requiring no pursuit—bees and butterflies on ice, and many spicy beetles, a

They flutter around
the explorer with the
liveliest curiosity, and come down
a little way, sometimes nearly a
mile, to meet him and conduct
him into their icy homes.

perpetual feast, on tables big for guests so small, and in vast banqueting halls ventilated by cool breezes that ruffle the feathers of the fairy brownies. Happy fellows, no rivals come to dispute possession with them. No other birds, not even hawks, as far as I have noticed, live so high. They see people so seldom, they flutter around the explorer with the liveliest curiosity, and come down a little way, sometimes nearly a mile, to meet him and conduct him into their icy homes.

When I was exploring the Merced group, climbing up the grand canyon between the Merced and Red Mountains into the fountain amphitheater of an ancient glacier, just as I was approaching the small active glacier that leans back in the shadow of Merced Mountain, a flock of twenty or thirty of these little birds, the first I had seen, came down the canyon to meet me, flying low, straight toward me as if they meant to fly in my face. Instead of attacking me or passing by, they circled round my head, chirping and fluttering for a minute or two, then turned and escorted me up the canyon, alighting on the nearest rocks on either hand, and flying ahead a few yards at a time to keep even with me.

SQUIRREL

One calm, creamy Indian summer morning, when the nuts were ripe, I was camped in the upper pine-woods of the south fork of the San Joaquin, where the squirrels seemed to be about as plentiful as the ripe burs. They were taking an early breakfast before going to their regular harvest-work....

Breakfast done, I whistled a tune for him [a squirrel] before he went to work, curious to see how he would be affected by it. He had not seen me all this while; but the instant I began to whistle he darted up the tree nearest to him, and came out on a small dead limb opposite me, and composed himself to listen. I sang and whistled more than a dozen airs, and as the music changed his eyes sparkled, and he turned his head quickly from side to side, but made no other response. Other squirrels, hearing the strange sounds, came around on all sides, also chipmunks and birds. One of the birds, a handsome, speckle-breasted thrush, seemed even more interested than the squirrels. After listening for a while on one of the lower dead sprays of a pine, he came swooping forward within a few feet of my face, and remained fluttering in the air for half a minute or so, sustaining himself with whirring wing-beats, like a hummingbird in front of a flower, while I could look into his eyes and see his innocent wonder.

By this time my performance must have lasted nearly half an hour. I sang or whistled "Bonnie Doon," "Lass o' Gowrie," "O'er the Water to Charlie," "Bonnie Woods o' Cragie Lee," etc., all of which seemed to be listened to with bright interest, my first Douglas sitting patiently through it all, with his telling eyes fixed upon me until I ventured to give the "Old Hundredth," when he screamed his Indian name, Pillil-looeet, turned tail, and darted with ludicrous haste up the tree out of sight, his voice and actions in the case leaving a somewhat profane impression, as if he had said, "I'll be hanged if you get me to hear anything so solemn and unpiny." This acted as a signal for the general dispersal of the whole hairy tribe, though the birds seemed willing to wait further developments, music being naturally more in their line.

What there can be in that grand old church tune that is so offensive to birds and squirrels I can't imagine. A year or two after this High Sierra concert, I was sitting one fine day on a hill in the Coast Range where the common ground squirrels were abundant. They were very shy on account of being hunted so much; but after I had been silent and motionless for half an hour or so they began to venture out of their holes and to feed on the seeds of the grasses and thistles around me as if I were no more to be feared than a tree stump. Then it occurred to me that this was a good opportunity to find out whether they also disliked "Old Hundredth." Therefore I began to whistle as nearly as I could remember the same familiar airs that had pleased the mountaineers of the Sierra. They at once stopped eating, stood erect, and listened patiently until I came to "Old Hundredth," when with ludicrous haste every one of them rushed to their holes and bolted in, their feet twinkling in the air for a moment as they vanished.

DOUGLAS SQUIRREL

One never tires of this bright chip of nature—this brave little voice crying in the wilderness—of observing his many works and ways, and listening to his curious language. His musical, piny gossip is as savory to the ear as balsam to the palate; and, though he has not exactly the gift of song, some of his notes are as sweet as those of a linnet—almost flute-like in softness, while others prick and tingle like thistles. He is the mockingbird of squirrels, pouring forth mixed chatter and song like a perennial fountain; barking like a dog, screaming like a hawk, chirping like a blackbird or a sparrow; while in bluff, audacious noisiness he is a very jay.

In descending the trunk of a tree with the intention of alighting on the ground, he preserves a cautious silence, mindful, perhaps, of foxes and wildcats; but while rocking safely at home in the pine-tops there is no end to his capers and noise; and woe to the gray squirrel or chipmunk that ventures to set foot on his favorite tree! No matter how slyly they trace the furrows of the bark, they are speedily discovered, and kicked downstairs with comic vehemence, while a torrent of angry notes comes rushing from his whiskered lips that sounds remarkably like swearing. He will even attempt at times to drive away dogs and men, especially if he has had no previous knowledge of them. Seeing a man for the first time, he approaches nearer and nearer, until within a few feet; then, with an angry outburst, he makes a sudden rush, all teeth and eyes, as if about to eat you up. But, finding that the big, forked animal doesn't scare, he prudently beats a retreat, and sets himself up to reconnoiter on some overhanging branch, scrutinizing every movement you make with ludicrous solemnity.

Gathering courage, he ventures down the trunk again, churring and chirping, and jerking nervously up and down in curious loops, eyeing you all the time, as if showing off and demanding your admiration. Finally, growing calmer, he settles down in a comfortable posture on some horizontal branch commanding a good view, and beats time with his tail to a steady "Chee-up! chee-up!" or, when somewhat less excited, "Pee-ah!" with the first syllable keenly accented, and the second drawn out like the scream of a hawk— repeating this slowly and more emphatically at first, then gradually faster, until a rate of about 150 words a minute is reached; usually sitting all the time on his haunches, with paws resting on his breast, which pulses visibly with each word. It is remarkable, too, that, though articulating distinctly, he keeps his mouth shut most of the time, and speaks through his nose. I have occasionally observed him even eating sequoia seeds and nibbling a troublesome flea, without ceasing or in any way confusing his "Pee-ah! pee-ah!" for a single moment.

WATER OUZEL

The water ouzel, in his rocky home amid foaming
waters, seldom sees a gun, and of all the singers I
like him the best. He is a plainly dressed little bird,
about the size of a robin, with short, crisp, but rather broad wings, and a tail of moderate length, slanted
up, giving him, with his nodding, bobbing manners,
a wrennish look. He is usually seen fluttering about
in the spray of falls and the rapid cascading portions
of the main branches of the rivers. These are his favorite haunts; but he is often seen also on comparatively level reaches and occasionally on the shores of
mountain lakes, especially at the beginning of winter,
when heavy snowfalls have blurred the streams with
sludge. Though not a waterbird in structure, he gets
his living in the water, and is never seen away from
the immediate margin of streams. He dives fearlessly

into rough, boiling eddies and rapids to feed at the bottom, flying underwater seemingly as easily as in the air. Sometimes he wades in shallow places, thrusting his head under from time to time in a nodding, frisky way that is sure to attract attention. His flight is a solid whir of wing-beats like that of a partridge, and in going from place to place along his favorite string of rapids he follows the windings of the stream, and usually alights on some rock or snag on the bank or out in the current, or rarely on the dry limb of an overhanging tree, perching like a tree bird when it suits his convenience. He has the oddest, neatest manners imaginable, and all his gestures as he flits about in the wild, dashing waters bespeak the utmost cheerfulness and confidence. He sings both winter and summer, in all sorts of weather—a sweet, fluty melody, rather low, and much less keen and accentuated than from the brisk vigor of his movements one would be led to expect.

How romantic and beautiful is the life of this brave little singer on the wild mountain streams, building his round bossy nest of moss by the side of a rapid or fall, where it is sprinkled and kept fresh and green by the spray! No wonder he sings well, since all the air about him is music; every breath he draws is part of a song, and he gets his first music lessons before he is born; for the eggs vibrate in time with the tones of the waterfalls. Bird and stream are inseparable, songful and wild, gentle and strong—the bird ever in danger in the midst of the stream's mad whirlpools, yet seemingly immortal. And so I might go on, writing words, words, words; but to what purpose? Go see him and love him, and through him as through a window, look into Nature's warm heart.

WOLF

I greatly enjoyed the Indian's campfire talk this
evening on their ancient customs, how they were
taught by their parents ere the whites came among
them, their religion, ideas connected with the next
world, the stars, plants, the behavior and language
of animals under different circumstances, manner
of getting a living, etc. When our talk was inter-
rupted by the howling of a wolf on the opposite
side of the strait, Kadachan puzzled the minister
with the question, "Have wolves souls?" The Indians believe that they have, giving as foundation for
their belief that they are wise creatures who know
how to catch seals and salmon by swimming slyly
upon them with their heads hidden in a mouthful
of grass, hunt deer in company, and always bring
forth their young at the same and most favorable

"Have wolves souls?"
The Indians believe
that they have.

time of the year. I inquired how it was that with enemies so wise and powerful the deer were not all killed. Kadachan replied that wolves knew better than to kill them all and thus cut off their most important food supply. He said they were numerous on all the large islands, more so than on the mainland, that Indian hunters were afraid of them and never ventured far into the woods alone, for these large gray and black wolves attacked man whether they were hungry or not. When attacked, the Indian hunter, he said, climbed a tree or stood with his back against a tree or rock, as a wolf never attacks face to face.

WOOD RAT

Neotoma is scarcely at all like the common rat, is nearly twice as large, has a delicate, soft, brownish fur, white on the belly, large ears thin and translucent, eyes full and liquid and mild in expression, nose blunt and squirrelish, slender claws sharp as needles, and as his limbs are strong he can climb about as well as a squirrel; while no rat or squirrel has so innocent a look, is so easily approached, or in general expresses so much confidence in one's good intentions. He seems too fine for the thorny thickets he inhabits, and his big, rough hut is as unlike himself as possible. No other animal in these mountains makes nests so large and striking in appearance as his. They are built of all kinds of sticks (broken branches, and old rotten moss-grown chunks and green twigs, smooth or thorny, cut from the nearest bushes), mixed with miscellaneous rubbish and curious odds and ends—bits of cloddy earth, stones, bones, bits of deer-horn, etc.: the whole simply piled in conical masses on the ground in chaparral thickets. Some of these cabins are five or six feet high, and occasionally a dozen or more are grouped together; less, perhaps, for society's sake than for advantages of food and shelter.

Coming through deep, stiff chaparral in the heart of the wilderness, heated and weary in forcing a way, the solitary explorer, happening into one of these curious neotoma villages, is startled at the strange sight, and may imagine he is in an Indian village, and feel anxious as to the reception he will get in a place so wild. At first, perhaps, not a single inhabitant will be seen, or at most only two or three seated on the tops of their huts as at the doors, observing the stranger with the mildest of mild eyes. The nest in the center of the cabin is made of grass and films of bark chewed to tow, and lined with feathers and the down of various seeds. The thick, rough walls seem to be built for defense against enemies—fox, coyote, etc.—as well as for shelter, and the delicate creatures in their big, rude homes, suggest tender flowers, like those of *Salvia carduacea,* defended by thorny involucres.

Sometimes the home is built in the forks of an oak, twenty or thirty feet from the ground, and even in garrets. Among housekeepers who have these bushmen as neighbors or guests, they are regarded as thieves, because they carry away and pile together everything transportable (knives, forks, tin cups, spoons, spectacles, combs, nails, kindling-wood, etc., as well as eatables of all sorts), to strengthen their fortifications or to shine among rivals. Once, far back in the high Sierra, they stole my snow goggles, the lid of my teapot, and my aneroid barometer; and one stormy night, when encamped under a prostrate cedar, I was awakened by a gritting sound on the granite, and by the light of my fire I discovered a handsome neotoma beside me, dragging away my ice hatchet, pulling with might and main by a buckskin string on the handle. I threw bits of bark at him and made a noise to frighten him, but he stood scolding and chattering back at me, his fine eyes shining with an air of injured innocence.

WOODCHUCK

In the spring of 1875, when I was exploring the peaks and glaciers about the head of the middle fork of the San Joaquin, I had crossed the range from the head of Owen River, and one morning, passing around a frozen lake where the snow was perhaps ten feet deep, I was surprised to find the fresh track of a woodchuck plainly marked, the sun having softened the surface. What could the animal be thinking of, coming out so early while all the ground was snow-buried? The steady trend of his track showed he had a definite aim, and fortunately it was toward a mountain thirteen thousand feet high that I meant to climb. So I followed to see if I could find out what he was up to. From the base of the mountain the track pointed straight up, and I knew by the melting snow that I was not far behind him. I lost the track on a crumbling ridge, partly

How did he know the
way to this one garden
spot, so high and far off,
and what told him that it
was in bloom while yet the
snow was ten feet deep
over his den?

projecting through the snow, but soon discovered it again. Well toward the summit of the mountain, in an open spot on the south side, nearly inclosed by disintegrating pinnacles among which the sun heat reverberated, making an isolated patch of warm climate, I found a nice garden, full of rock cress, phlox, silene, draba, etc., and a few grasses; and in this garden I overtook the wanderer, enjoying a fine fresh meal, perhaps the first of the season. How did he know the way to this one garden spot, so high and far off, and what told him that it was in bloom while yet the snow was ten feet deep over his den? For this it would seem he would need more botanical, topographical, and climatological knowledge than most mountaineers are possessed of.

Sources

Bear, Clarke crow, deer, grouse, rattlesnake, sparrow, water ouzel, wood rat, and woodchuck stories from *Our National Parks* (1901).

Bee, wild sheep, squirrel, and Douglas squirrel stories from *The Mountains of California* (1894).

Ant, grasshopper, and domestic sheep stories from *My First Summer in the Sierra* (1911).

Raven, salmon, and wolf stories from *Travels in Alaska* (1915).

Golden eagle and lizard stories from *The Life and Letters of John Muir,* volume II, edited by William Frederic Badè. © 1924 by Houghton Mifflin Company, renewed 1952 by John Muir Hanna. Used with permission of Houghton Mifflin Harcourt Publishing Company. All rights reserved.

Goose and mouse stories from *The Story of My Boyhood and Youth* (1913).

Eagle/hare and heron stories from *A Thousand-Mile Walk to the Gulf* (1916).

Songbird story ("Protect Our Songbirds") is a clipping found in Muir's files probably from *The San Francisco Examiner* sometime in the spring of 1895. Reprinted from *The John Muir Newsletter,* volume 1, number 4, fall 1991. A publication of the John Muir Papers, Holt-Atherton Special Collections, University of the Pacific. © 1984 Muir-Hanna Trust. Used with permission.

Dog story from *Stickeen* (1909).

The following books helped inspire this collection: *Muir among the Animals,* by Lisa Mighetto (Sierra Club Books, 1986); *Mark Twain's Book of Animals,* edited by Shelley Fisher Fishkin (UC Press, 2011); and *A California Bestiary,* by Rebecca Solnit and Mona Caron (Heyday, 2010). Heyday also thanks The John Muir Exhibit of the Sierra Club for easy access to Muir's writings.

About Heyday

Heyday is an independent, nonprofit publisher and unique cultural institution. We promote widespread awareness and celebration of California's many cultures, landscapes, and boundary-breaking ideas. Through our well-crafted books, public events, and innovative outreach programs we are building a vibrant community of readers, writers, and thinkers.

Thank You

It takes the collective effort of many to create a thriving literary culture. We are thankful to all the thoughtful people we have the privilege to engage with. Cheers to our writers, artists, editors, storytellers, designers, printers, bookstores, critics, cultural organizations, readers, and book lovers everywhere!

We are especially grateful for the generous funding we've received for our publications and programs during the past year from foundations and hundreds of individual donors. Major supporters include:

Alliance for California Traditional Arts; Anonymous (6); Arkay Foundation; Judith and Phillip Auth; Judy Avery; Carol Baird and Alan Harper; Paul Bancroft III; The Bancroft Library; Richard and Rickie Ann Baum; BayTree Fund; S. D. Bechtel, Jr. Foundation; Jean and Fred Berensmeier; Berkeley Civic Arts Program and Civic Arts Commission; Joan Berman; Nancy Bertelsen; Barbara Boucke; Beatrice Bowles, in memory of Susan S. Lake; John Briscoe; David Brower Center; Lewis and Sheana Butler; Helen Cagampang; California Historical Society; California Indian Heritage Center Foundation; California State Parks Foundation; Joanne Campbell; The Campbell Foundation; James and Margaret Chapin; Graham Chisholm; The Christensen Fund; Jon Christensen; Cynthia Clarke; Community Futures Collective; Lawrence Crooks; Lauren and Alan Dachs; Nik Dehejia; Topher Delaney; Chris Desser and Kirk Marckwald; Lokelani Devone; Frances Dinkelspiel and Gary Wayne; Doune Fund; The Durfee Foundation; Megan

Fletcher and J.K. Dineen; Michael Eaton and Charity Kenyon; Richard and Gretchen Evans; Flow Fund Circle; Friends of the Roseville Library; Furthur Foundation; The Wallace Alexander Gerbode Foundation; Patrick Golden; Nicola W. Gordon; Wanda Lee Graves and Stephen Duscha; The Walter and Elise Haas Fund; Coke and James Hallowell; Theresa Harlan and Ken Tiger; Cindy Heitzman; Carla Hills; Sandra and Charles Hobson; Nettie Hoge; Donna Ewald Huggins; JiJi Foundation; Claudia Jurmain; Kalliopeia Foundation; Lowry and Croul; Marty and Pamela Krasney; Robert and Karen Kustel; Guy Lampard and Suzanne Badenhoop; Thomas Lockard and Alix Marduel; Thomas J. Long Foundation; Bryce Lundberg; Sam and Alfreda Maloof Foundation for Arts & Crafts; Michael McCone; Giles W. and Elise G. Mead Foundation; Moore Family Foundation; Michael J. Moratto, in memory of Major J. Moratto; Stewart R. Mott Foundation; The MSB Charitable Fund; Karen and Thomas Mulvaney; Richard Nagler; National Wildlife Federation; Native Arts and Cultures Foundation; Humboldt Area Foundation, Native Cultures Fund; The Nature Conservancy; Nightingale Family Foundation; Steven Nightingale and Lucy Blake; Northern California Water Association; Ohlone-Costanoan Esselen Nation; Panta Rhea Foundation; David Plant; Jean Pokorny; Steven Rasmussen and Felicia Woytak; Restore Hetch Hetchy; Robin Ridder; Spreck and Isabella Rosekrans; Alan Rosenus; The San Francisco Foundation; Toby and Sheila Schwartzburg; Sierra College; Stephen M. Silberstein Foundation; Ernest and June Siva, in honor of the Dorothy Ramon Learning Center; Carla Soracco; John and Beverly Stauffer Foundation; Radha Stern, in honor of Malcolm Margolin and Diane Lee; Roselyne Chroman Swig; TomKat Charitable Trust; Tides Foundation; Sonia Torres; Michael and Shirley Traynor; The Roger J. and Madeleine Traynor Foundation; Lisa Van Cleef and Mark Gunson; Patricia Wakida; John Wiley & Sons, Inc.; Peter Booth Wiley and Valerie Barth; Bobby Winston; Dean Witter Foundation; Yocha Dehe Wintun Nation; and Yosemite Conservancy.

BOARD OF DIRECTORS

GETTING INVOLVED

To learn more about our publications, events, membership club, and other ways you can participate, please visit www.heydaybooks.com.